# Preparing the Eucharistic Table

*Barry Glendinning*

NOVALIS
THE LITURGICAL PRESS
EJ DWYER

Design: Eye-to-Eye Design, Toronto

Layout: Suzanne Latourelle

Illustrations: Eugene Kral

Series Editor: Bernadette Gasslein

Scripture quotations from the New Revised Standard Version of the Bible, © 1989, Division of Christian Education of the National Council of Churches of Christ in the United States. Used with permission.

© 1996, Novalis, Saint Paul University, Ottawa, ON, Canada

Business Office: Novalis, 49 Front Street East, 2nd floor, Toronto, ON  M5E 1B3

Novalis: ISBN 2-89088-795-2

The Liturgical Press: ISBN 0-8146-2482-0
A Liturgical Press Book
Published in the United States of America by The Liturgical Press, Collegeville, Minnesota 56321

EJ Dwyer: ISBN 0-85574-071-X
EJ Dwyer, Locked Bag 71, Alexandria, NSW 2015, Australia

Printed in Canada.

Canadian Cataloguing in Publication Data

Glendinning, Barry
        Preparing the Eucharistic table

(Preparing for liturgy)
        Includes bibliographical references.
        ISBN 2-89088-795-2

        1. Lord's Supper (Liturgy) 2. Lord's Supper—
Catholic Church. 3. Catholic Church—Liturgy. I. Title.
II. Series.

BX2215.2G64 1997 264'.02036      C96-900892-9

# Contents

# Introduction

Sometimes in our reflective moments we cast our eyes back to the time when Jesus walked the dusty roads of Galilee and Judea. We remember the table fellowship that was so much a part of his earthly journey. Bethany was a favourite resting place, and Martha, Mary and Lazarus must have experienced a special joy as Jesus sat at table with them. On a wider scale, we remember the miraculous feeding of the thousands and the compassion that Jesus had for the crowd. Most of all we wonder what it would have been like to be with him at the Last Supper, to converse with him, to share the food and drink, to experience his presence and his love.

No doubt Jesus' disciples greatly appreciated being with him at the table. And, given recent events, they probably sensed that some real danger lay ahead. Yet, despite what Jesus had told them, they had only a vague inkling of what was going to happen. They could scarcely grasp that he would die and rise from the dead, that he would ascend to the right hand of the Father, exalted as the Lord of the universe, and that he would draw all things to himself through the power of the Holy Spirit.

This kind of reflection is good for us all, but only if it opens out the marvels of the present moment, only if it helps us see more clearly what the Lord is doing for us today. Today the Lord is present in our midst, completing the work that he has already begun. This was his promise: "And remember, I am with you always, to the end of the age" (Mt 28:20).

Only when we remember that the risen and exalted Lord is among us can we begin to look for signs of his presence. Then our eyes are drawn to the Sunday eucharist, the special ground of encounter. Here the Lord welcomes the people of the world, speaks to them from the heart and invites them to gather at table with him.

This is why those who prepare liturgy should priorize the Sunday celebration. They do not create the event, but they do facilitate the encounter. In the liturgy of the word, they ensure that the Lord's message is proclaimed with living faith in the midst of the church. In the liturgy of the eucharist, they set a festive table of the Lord.

*Preparing the Table of the Word*, another booklet in this series, provides an in-depth look at the liturgy of the word. This booklet has the liturgy of the eucharist as its special focus.

It presents the remarkable picture of the liturgy of the eucharist as the feast of God's kingdom. This picture reveals how the Lord sets a festive table in our midst, inviting us all to share the food and drink of everlasting life. Our fond reflections and deepest yearnings are fulfilled today as the Lord gathers us to himself, inviting us, as the liturgy of Easter Sunday proclaims, "to feast with joy in the Lord. Alleluia."

This booklet explores this deeper meaning of the Lord's table and provides many suggestions for effective celebration. Parish liturgy planners, presiders, liturgical ministers, and everyone who celebrates the Sunday eucharist will find here a combination of theory and practice, of vision and application that will help them prepare the table of the Lord with grace and joy.

# CHAPTER 1

# The Liturgy of the Eucharist

## The Church's Great Feast

The best way to explore the liturgy of the eucharist is to let a few traditional questions lead us in some unexpected directions:

- What is the liturgy of the eucharist?

- Who celebrates it?

- Why do we celebrate it?

- Where do we celebrate it?

- When do we celebrate it?

- How do we celebrate it?

## What is the Liturgy of the Eucharist?

The liturgy of the eucharist is the church's sacred meal. It is a meal, complete with table, food and drink, and invited guests. It is a sacred meal that draws the participants into communion of life with the all-holy God. Masterfully designed for the whole of creation, it has the potential and the power to be the world's great feast.

Here are some important things that we say about the feast. Each expresses the same reality and truth in one distinctive way.

• The liturgy of the eucharist is a thanksgiving meal. Eucharist means *thanksgiving*. The table blessing, the eucharistic prayer, is an exalted prayer that gives thanks to God for the salvation that the world experiences through the death and resurrection of Jesus Christ.

• The liturgy of the eucharist is a *sacrificial meal*. In the eucharistic prayer the church recalls Jesus in his sacrificial death and resurrection; by the power of the Holy Spirit the food and drink become the very presence of Christ in his sacrifice.

• The liturgy of the eucharist is a *passover meal*. It celebrates the saving passage of Jesus from death to resurrected and exalted life. Those who share the body and blood of Christ journey with him through death to the freedom and joy of new life.

• The liturgy of the eucharist is a *kingdom meal*. It joins heaven and earth, offering the world communion of life with God in the body and blood of Christ.

• The liturgy of the eucharist is a *covenant meal*. It celebrates the new covenant of love that is sealed in the Lord's death and resurrection. In the eucharistic prayer, the assembled church offers its life to God in Jesus Christ: "Through him, with him, in him, in the unity of the Holy Spirit, all glory and honour is yours, almighty Father, for ever and ever. Amen." Sharing holy communion, it seals the covenant in the body and blood of Christ.

## Liturgy planners can ...

• ensure that the celebration stands out boldly as a sacred meal. Centuries of change tended to obscure the true identity of the liturgy of the eucharist as the Lord's supper, the church's festive meal.

• place a table worthy of the feast in the midst of the assembly and set it with a plate of tasty bread and a generous cup of wine for all to share. This is the finest way to shape the sacred meal!

## *Who Celebrates It?*

The answer to this question reveals an astounding feature of the church's sacred meal: the whole world is invited to the feast! God calls everybody in every age to the end of time to gather there.

The eucharist is the centrepiece of God's plan to reconcile the world in Christ. When we grasp its extraordinary scope, we catch a glimpse of all the peoples and nations of the world gathered together at one table, partaking of one holy food and drink, and sharing one new life in God.

The Sunday assembly, then, is a truly remarkable sight. It includes the rich and the poor, the young and the old. It embraces people of every language and culture, every colour of skin, every political affiliation, every position in society. It is the striking picture of a world brought together by the Holy Spirit at the one table of the Lord. Here is God's new creation.

## Liturgy planners can ...

• make genuine hospitality at the doors a top priority.

• encourage the community to gather freely and greet one another warmly before the celebration begins. See if you can create a warm and generous space to facilitate this.

• try to arrange the interior space so that the community can gather as a household around the Lord's table.

• avoid so-called children's masses and the like on Sunday. Every Sunday eucharist should be the gathering of the new household of God; the way we celebrate every Sunday eucharist should take into account the rich diversity of the assembly.

• encourage a celebration that displays the radical nature of the feast: the one table of the Lord, the one bread that becomes the body of Christ broken and shared by all; the one cup of wine that becomes the blood of Christ poured out for all; the new assembly gathered in the unity and peace of God.

## Why Do We Celebrate Eucharist?

We might turn the question around and put it this way: "Why did the Lord give us the feast?" The answer is clear: to draw us into communion of life with the triune God.

If the answer is clear, it is also overwhelming. It takes us beyond formulas and definitions into the marvellous and unrelenting love of a God who says to the whole world: "I love you deeply. My great desire is to have you with me. Come, sing and dance and rejoice with me. Come, share my life forever!"

As we try to come to terms with such unbounded love, it is good for us to remember how close God has come to us in the person of Jesus Christ. In Matthew, he is called Emmanuel, "which means, 'God is with us'" (1:23). Jesus walked through life with his disciples. Particularly striking is that he sat at table again and again with sinners. Jesus was the Father's gracious invitation to a broken and fallen world to share communion of life with the all-holy God.

Is it so surprising, then, that the risen and exalted Lord would set a festive table in our midst, host a banquet for the whole world and offer us the food and drink of everlasting life?

### Liturgy planners can ...

• keep in mind that the eucharistic celebration is the Lord's work. The risen and exalted Christ hosts the sacred meal; he invites the guests and works wonders in their midst. Your work is not to create liturgical celebrations. Rather, it is to facilitate what the Lord has in mind.

You may observe that the assembly sometimes fails to recognize that it is the Lord himself who presides at the church's eucharist. Perhaps too singular an emphasis on the real and substantial presence of Christ in the eucharistic food and drink has obscured the real presence of Christ in every dimension of the celebration. The church found it necessary to defend the real presence of Christ in the consecrated food and drink in the face of those who openly disclaimed it, with the result that it became the sole focus of our attention. In the process, we lost sight of the wider picture. Article seven of the *Constitution on the Sacred*

*Liturgy* reminds us that Christ is truly present in the minister who presides, in the word that is proclaimed, in the gathered people themselves, "but especially under the eucharistic elements."

## Where Do We Celebrate It?

The easy answer to this question is that the eucharist takes place in a church building. But the far more significant observation is that it takes place in the world. Even this response seems to be perfectly obvious and transparent; yet a few distinctions may prove our assumptions wrong.

Long ago it was customary to divide the world into two rather distinct compartments: the sacred and the profane. The ancient temple stood as the place of God's dwelling; everything outside the temple was profane (from *pro-fanum*, meaning before or outside the temple).

But Jesus brought the living presence of God into the whole world. He walked the roads of Galilee and Judea and sat at table with his friends. His sacrifice, the gift of his own life for the world, took place outside the temple and beyond Jerusalem on a "profane" hill. And when God raised him from death and drew him to his right hand, Jesus sent the Holy Spirit with power to transform the world and draw it within the holiness of the living God.

In the age of the Holy Spirit, the community gathered for eucharist is itself the new temple of God: "For we are the temple of the living God, as God said, 'I will live in them and walk among them, and I will be their God, and they shall be my people'" (2 Cor 6:16). Through the power of the Holy Spirit, we "are built together spiritually into a dwelling place for God" (Eph 2:22).

In fact, the assembly gathers the whole world into its prayer, so that the entire universe dances in communion with the God of creation and becomes one grand temple of the Spirit. Our liturgy, then, does not take place in a sacred enclave. It is set in the midst of the world which the prayer of the church declares as sacred space.

### Liturgy planners can ...

• discuss ways to connect the church's liturgy with the whole of life. Perhaps you have spotted the modern version of the sacred versus the profane. It is the idea that Christians "go to church" on Sunday to pay their respects to God and then spend the rest of the week going about their own business. This amounts to the separation of liturgy and life. Only when we see liturgy as the world dancing in communion with its God do liturgy and life become one.

• celebrate this sacred meal in a way that enables everyone to recognize it as a worldly, domestic event. The fundamental connection between liturgy and life is the meal itself, a domestic event grounded in our "worldly" life. When Jesus chose a meal as the centrepiece of our communion with God, he grounded liturgy solidly in the world. Perhaps we have unwittingly contributed to the separation of liturgy and life by letting the sacred meal stray too far from ordinary life: a table that doesn't resemble a table, bread that doesn't look like bread, and a meal that doesn't seem to be a meal.

• discuss how a fresh focus would change your approach to the celebration. We have sometimes overlooked the fact that the assembly is the new and living temple of the Holy Spirit. We have paid more attention to the church building and its appointments than to the temple that is no longer built of stones. Make sure, for example, that the building serves the assembly and its liturgy of praise. Surround the assembly with festive decorations: the people are the new sanctuary of God.

## *When Do We Celebrate It?*

The church's principal and normative eucharist takes place on Sunday. Sometimes, however, we fail to explore why Sunday and the celebration of the eucharist coincide.

Sunday is the day of Christ's resurrection, the day of his exaltation as Lord of the universe, and the day of the dramatic descent of the Holy Spirit upon the world. Sunday marks the start of the new creation, the opening-out of the reign of God, the beginning of the age of fulfilment. This is why Christians call this day the Lord's Day.

The eucharist, which is proper to the Lord's Day, is essential to it because eucharist announces, reveals, and makes present the new creation. The sacred meal bridges heaven and earth. It is the revelation of the banquet feast of the kingdom. Its table, at which the Lord of glory presides, is set with the food and drink of new and everlasting life, the body and blood of Christ.

The image of God's kingdom given us by Matthew springs to mind: "The kingdom of heaven may be compared to a king who gave a wedding banquet for his son" (Mt 22:2). And we will remember the parable of the great dinner, recorded in Luke, where one of the guests exclaims, "Blessed is anyone who will eat bread in the kingdom of God!" (Lk 14:15).

What is truly amazing is that the Lord who has set the table of the kingdom feast in our midst has invited the world to partake of its life-giving food and drink. The liturgy itself expresses this remarkable truth in its thanksgiving prayer when it proclaims, "Now, with angels and archangels, and the whole company of heaven, we sing the unending hymn of your praise: Holy, holy, holy Lord, God of power and might, heaven and earth are full of your glory. Hosanna in the highest. Blessed is he who comes in the name of the Lord. Hosanna in the highest."

This extraordinary dimension of the eucharist is what makes the sacred meal so precious in the eyes of Christians and so grand a cause for joyful celebration.

## Liturgy planners can ...

• try to make joy the special characteristic of the great feast. In his farewell discourse, Jesus said to his disciples, "I have said these things to you so that my joy may be in you, and that your joy may be complete" (Jn 15:11). Help the Christian community to recognize the presence of the exalted Lord and the arrival of the banquet of the kingdom.

• encourage ministers to smile. Provide the assembly with festive songs of praise, and let the alleluias ring.

• ensure that processions declare the images and the joy of kingdom life. Examine the movement of your processions. Do the ministers move with energy and grace? People in the community who are skilled in the art of movement can help transform stodgy processions into actions that reveal the transforming presence of the Lord. Examine your processional cross. Does it really convey the victory of the triumphant Christ? Examine your book of the gospels. Does it reflect the glory of Jesus and his kingdom? Examine the presider's vesture. Does it capture the splendour of the church's new life?

## *How Do We Celebrate It?*

The world's finest meal calls for the finest kind of celebration. The following chapters provide liturgy planners, presiders, liturgical ministers, and the whole assembly with detailed and step-by-step suggestions for preparing the Christian community's celebration of the feast of feasts.

## *In Summary*

1. The eucharist is the feast of feasts. Set in the midst of the world, its goal is to gather the whole of creation into the kingdom of God.

2. The Lord invites us to dine with him, and presides at the table.

3. From Lord's Day to Lord's Day, this high festival draws us into the celebration of the fullness of life in God.

## *Discussion Questions*

1. What do you find most striking about the way that the liturgy of the eucharist is described in this chapter?

2. The liturgy of the eucharist is a kingdom feast. In what way does it reveal and express the presence of the kingdom in our midst?

3. The goal of the eucharist is to unite the world in one sacred meal. Describe the diverse makeup of your parish Sunday assembly.

4. "The world's finest meal calls for the finest kind of celebration." Does your parish eucharist reach the level of genuine celebration?

# CHAPTER 2

# Preparing the Altar and the Gifts: Setting the Lord's Table

In ordinary language, we can describe this part of the liturgy as setting the table for the feast. We all know that a lot of painstaking preparation goes on behind the scenes before any important celebration takes place. A menu has to be drawn up; food has to be purchased and prepared. A festive table cloth and appropriate tableware have to be selected and set out. The Christian community does a similar thing in preparation for its sacred meal.

## The Menu

The menu for the Lord's supper is, at least at first sight, quite straightforward. It is bread and wine, the staple food and drink of life, which in the course of the sacred meal will be transformed by the Spirit into the body and blood of Christ.

You can do a number of things to improve the bread and wine that we use for the eucharistic banquet. At the most basic level, the bread used for the eucharist should look like real bread; it should be bread that can be broken for the assembly during the rite that we call "the breaking of bread." Enough wine to serve the entire assembly should be used in the sacred meal.

## Liturgy planners can ...

• discuss the possibility of organizing a team of parishioners to bake bread for the eucharist.

A lot of background preparation will be required so that the bread eventually introduced into the liturgy follows the prescriptions of liturgical law, is attractive, breaks readily, does not crumble and is easily consumed.

For the past thousand years, the Western church has used unleavened bread; that practice remains in force today. The bread must be baked using only flour and water. It may be scored, preferably on the bottom, to facilitate breaking. It can be prepared in various portions and frozen until use.

One proven recipe for eucharistic bread is on the next page. It can serve as a starting point for experienced bakers who will continue to work on the project.

• discuss the possibility of making your own wine. This kind of hands-on preparation of the food and drink draws the community closer to the basic symbols of the sacred meal. The wine used for the Lord's supper is made from the fermented and unfortified juice of the grape.

• closely scrutinize the tableware the community uses for its meal.

The plate for the bread should be large enough to hold all the bread that will be used for the celebration. This single plate of bread, sign of the unity of the assembly, is brought forward in procession. (A small amount of consecrated bread is reserved in the tabernacle, primarily for communion to the dying. It is used within the eucharistic celebration only in emergencies.)

The carafe for the wine should likewise be large enough to hold all the wine that will be needed for the celebration.

The cup or chalice should be a truly precious vessel. Traditionally, the cup and the book of the gospels are the community's most cherished possessions. Larger and larger cups were used as communities grew; the one cup remained a strong symbol of the unity of the people who gather at the table of the Lord.

If extra plates or cups are needed for a celebration, they, too, should be fitting for the feast.

Other articles used in conjunction with the Lord's table, such as the tablecloth and the candles, should be made of natural and authentic materials. An unbleached cloth and wax candles identify the celebration with creation, nature and the earth in ways that artificial materials cannot do.

## Eucharistic Bread

Ingredients

2/3 cup unbleached flour
1/3 cup  whole wheat flour
1/2 cup of unflavoured sparkling water

## Method

1. Preheat oven to 400$^0$ F (200$^0$ C). Spray a 9-inch (23 cm) pie plate with cooking spray and wipe off excess.

2. Mix the ingredients in a chilled bowl. Add more water if necessary to form a ball. Flatten the dough into the pie plate and score into 100 pieces.

3. Bake the bread for 15 minutes. Prick the top with a fork. Turn the loaf over and bake for 5 more minutes. Turn over again and bake for 5 minutes more.

4. Cool over a wire rack. Wrap tightly in plastic wrap and store in a plastic bag.

Note: The bread is best used as soon as possible, but it can be frozen for future use.

## How to Celebrate Well

Setting the table for a special meal is something that we do with particular care. We know that a table which is properly set and beautifully appointed charms the eyes and speaks its own language about the joy of the feast.

### Liturgy planners can ...

• keep the preparation rites simple, straightforward and clear. This will allow the table blessing of the eucharistic prayer and the eating and drinking of the communion rite to dominate the feast. Unfortunately, this is one of those suggestions that is more easily said than done. It requires first-class organization behind the scenes.

• prepare for setting the table. Setting the table at this time helps to mark the transition from the liturgy of the word to the liturgy of the eucharist. When everyone is seated after the general intercessions, servers or other members of the assembly spread the cloth on the table and light the candles. They also spread the corporal at the centre of the table and put the sacramentary in place. Additional lighting over the table can be turned on. All of this should be carried out in a unhurried and careful way.

• re-examine the collection and the presentation of the gifts.

*The collection.* If an adequate number of ministers are available to collect the community's monetary offerings, the collection can be taken up in one movement from front to back.

*The presentation of the gifts.* Liturgy planners can avoid most of the problems associated with the presentation of the gifts by inviting parishioners to volunteer for this ministry and by circulating a schedule as is done for other ministers. Hold a practice session with the volunteers and cover all the details: when to pick up the gifts, when to begin the procession, how to carry the bread and wine (so that the assembly can see them), and so on. See that those who are taking part in the procession make themselves ready during the setting of the table. Then the procession can begin without delay and the flow of the preparation rites will be maintained.

• make sure that the gifts are carried directly to the table. It is a good idea for the gift bearers to remain at the side of the table until the prayer over the gifts, which concludes the procession, has been prayed.

• keep the procession with the gifts simple. There is no need for cross and candles. Only the collection and the bread and wine should be carried forward. When other materials are carried in the procession they draw attention away from the proper objects of the rite.

• consider, at least on occasion, supplementing the monetary collection with other offerings for those in need. The Mass of the Lord's Supper on Holy Thursday is one of many opportunities to do this. On these occasions, the entire assembly may take part in the procession.

Sometimes you might ask ministers skilled in the art of movement to carry the gifts, showing them to the assembly on the way to the table.

• make sure that processions, festive by their very nature, can be described as the liturgical parades which they are. The procession with the gifts is no exception. Thus, a festive song of praise should accompany the liturgical action. And the gift bearers should move forward in a free and joyful manner.

## Music ministers can …

• refrain from any kind of music while the table is being set and the collection is being taken up. This allows the assembly to remained focused on the setting of the table and on the preparation of the gifts. The preparation time should not be viewed as a kind of pause in the liturgy when any "occasional" piece of music may be appropriate. Any elaborate musical presentation at this time would draw undue attention to this part of the celebration.

• lead the assembly in a processional song during the presentation of the gifts. The hymn spans the procession, beginning when it gets underway and concluding just before the prayer over the gifts. Try to select a hymn that has a sufficient number of verses, and allow for extra time when incense is used during this part of the celebration.

• choose a festive hymn that is suitable to accompany a procession. A general song of praise matches the occasion well.

## Presiders can ...

• try to emphasize the principal actions of the rite, namely taking the gifts and placing them on the table.

• receive the gifts at the table itself. (Remember: the prayers over the bread and the cup on the table are intended to be said silently. If there is no processional song, they may be said out loud.)

• incense the altar and the gifts, but not the cross, if you use incense at this time. Wait for the people to stand, and incense them as well.

## The whole assembly can ...

• sing the processional song.

• see itself as providing the food and drink of the sacred meal and the means to carry out the works of charity that flow from it.

• stand to be incensed if incense is used. Otherwise, stand before the invitation to the prayer over the gifts.

## *In Summary*

1. The first step in celebrating the liturgy of the eucharist is to set the table of the Lord. Not unlike our festive meals at home, this involves important preparations behind the scenes.

2. Arranging the table and presenting the gifts are important features of rite. When everything is done with planning and care, this part of the liturgy can be simple, clear and deeply impressive.

## *Discussion Questions*

1. Discuss how this part of the liturgy unfolds in your parish community. Do you set the table at this time? Do you have a simple yet expressive procession with the gifts? Do the gift bearers carry the bread and wine all the way to the altar?

2. Discuss the quality of the bread and wine that you use for the eucharist. Have you considered baking your own bread or making your own wine?

3. Discuss the quality of the plate(s) and cup(s) that are used in the celebration. Do they serve the feast well?

4. Discuss the style of music that you use to accompany this part of the eucharist. Is it the most suitable music that you can find? Does it continue until the presider has washed his hands?

# CHAPTER 3

# The Eucharistic Prayer: the Table Blessing of the Feast

The eucharistic prayer towers over the church's sacred meal. This rich and significant prayer deserves careful study by the whole community of faith. In the celebration itself, it needs to be proclaimed in the finest possible way; liturgy planners, presiders and the entire assembly will be interested in making that happen. We shall examine the eucharistic prayer under two principal headings:

- How to understand the eucharistic prayer;
- How to pray it well.

## How to Understand the Eucharistic Prayer

The first and most important thing that can be said about the eucharistic prayer is that it is the table blessing of the feast.

Table blessings are a prominent feature of our Judeo-Christian tradition. Whenever we eat and drink, we bless God, that is, we praise and thank God who has given us all good things. More than a mere formality, these table blessings bear witness to the fundamental truth that everything comes from God and belongs to God. Whenever we pray these blessings, we acknowledge God's sovereignty over all creation and we express our gratitude for God's gracious providence in our lives.

Four dimensions of the eucharistic prayer deserve particular attention. Although their titles are rather daunting, they expose the height and breadth and depth of what the early church simply called "the prayer."

### The ecclesial dimension

(from *ecclesia*, meaning assembly or church). The eucharistic prayer is the normative and fundamental faith-expression of the church, the ultimate mark of our identity as the people of God. When we pray this prayer we stand in solidarity with the church's assemblies throughout the world in every age.

### The cosmic dimension

(from *cosmos*, meaning world). In the eucharistic prayer, the assembly gathers the whole world into the praise of God. The table blessing becomes a cosmic prayer of praise, the hymn of the universe to God's glory. In this way, the whole world resonates once again in communion of life with its God.

### The pneumatic dimension

(from *pneuma*, meaning spirit). A dramatic feature of the church's eucharist is the presence and power of the Holy Spirit. The assembly prays the prayer in the power of the Spirit, offering praise and thanksgiving and consecrating its whole life and being to God. Through the power of the same Spirit the bread and wine over which the blessing is prayed are transformed into the body and blood of Christ.

### The eschatological dimension

(from *eschaton*, meaning the coming age). The eucharistic prayer joins the world to the everlasting prayer of Jesus, the great High Priest, who is seated in glory at the right hand of the Father. Together with the angels and saints, we pray the prayer of kingdom life, which is a prayer of everlasting praise and thanksgiving to the glory of God. The great prayer announces and reveals that God's reign has already broken into our world.

## How to Pray the Eucharistic Prayer Well

The eucharistic prayer is the most important prayer of the celebration; therefore, it needs to be proclaimed particularly well. Here are suggestions that will help make this prayer everything that it is called to be.

### Presiders can ...

• clearly understand the importance of the table blessing as the grand eucharistic prayer.

• make sure that it stands out from all other prayers that surround it. You might pause briefly before you begin the prayer and again after the great Amen. This gives the prayer an open and free space of its own. Pray it in a measured, proclamatory style.

• sing not only the preface but the rest of the prayer as well, since singing adds a special character to any text. This particular suggestion gives rise to a number of observations: 1) The eucharistic prayer is the prayer above all others that deserves to be sung; 2) many presiders, however, are either uncomfortable with singing alone or do not sing well; 3) yet almost everyone can learn to sing the chants well with a bit of help from parishioners who have received some voice training.

• be sure to recognize that the entire assembly prays the eucharistic prayer. You pray it in the name of Christ, the head of his body, the church; the whole body prays this prayer with him. Reach out to the assembly in the opening dialogue; make eye contact and use open and welcoming gestures. In this way the assembly will know that you are genuinely inviting it into the prayer. You can then keep your arms outstretched in the *orans* posture and attend to the careful enunciation of the text.

• move beyond the mere recitation of the text to pray the prayer from the heart. The eucharistic prayer has to become the authentic, living, embodied prayer of the people of God today. It has to be prayed with the conviction of faith. In order to prepare yourself to pray this prayer well, you will need some transition time between your other pastoral activities and the celebration of the eucharist. If you have more or less committed the prayer to memory, you will be able, in the course of the actual celebration, to shift your attention from the printed text to the fervour of the proclamation itself.

• spend some time outside the eucharist working on effectively proclaiming the prayer. Practice each sentence in a paragraph, emphasizing its key words. Then move on to the proper rhythm and phrasing of the paragraph itself. Finally, you can look at the broader rhythm and momentum of the whole prayer: separate each paragraph and section discretely and build the prayer into a complex whole. In a clear and nuanced way, the entire prayer should move forward to the closing doxology and the great Amen.

Integrating gestures and words so that the text continues to flow is a particular challenge. For example, you should practice picking up the plate of bread (and the cup, if there is no deacon) in preparation for the doxology without interrupting the proclamation of the prayer.

• make sure that your gestures are consistent with the liturgical moment. During the institution narrative and at the doxology, hold the bread or the cup about a handsbreadth above the table after the manner of a table blessing. During the institution narrative, do not mimic the acts of breaking and giving. Tailor your gesture to the size of the gathering and respect the overall flow of the prayer.

## Music ministers can ...

• give the acclamations of the eucharistic prayer your first attention; they are the primary sung parts of the eucharist.

• keep in mind that the eucharistic prayer belongs to the entire assembly. Always choose melodies that the assembly knows and that they can and will sing. Perhaps two sets of acclamations, alternated with the season, are all you need for a fairly long period of time.

• select a set of acclamations composed in an integrated manner. This supports the unity of the prayer.

• choose music that has strong intervals and an energetic melodic line for the acclamations, and sing it in a strong and vigorous style. A careful selection of organ stops and the additional use of various instruments, such as the trumpet in festal seasons, will enhance the celebratory character of the acclamations.

• ensure that the assembly can sing the acclamations of the eucharistic prayer even when adequate musical support is lacking.

• sing the acclamations without interrupting the natural flow and momentum of the prayer. Therefore, don't give the acclamations lengthy introductions. A single note serves best. If the presider sings the prayer, even this note should be unnecessary.

Let the great Amen, the most important of the acclamations of the eucharistic prayer, stand out above the others and punctuate the prayer with a dramatic close.

• make every effort to use additional acclamations provided for a eucharistic prayer, since they maintain the assembly's vocal involvement in the prayer. A cantor, who leads the community into the acclamation, may cue them.

• make the acclamations more brilliant at certain seasons by adding choral parts to the principal melodic line. But the music group should have such a command of their material that the leader does not need to direct them. If anything, the leader should invite the assembly into the acclamations by a gesture of the hand.

## The whole assembly can ...

• take ownership of the eucharistic prayer. Keep in mind that the prayer is consistently prayed in the plural form: for example, "Father, *we* celebrate the memory of Christ your Son."

• make the sentiments of the prayer your own as it is proclaimed. The eucharistic prayer is intended to be prayed with genuine fervour. Sing the acclamations with heartfelt praise to the glory of God.

• make the great Amen your personal, corporate, and public assent to everything that has been prayed.

## Liturgy planners can ...

• discuss the possibility of inviting the assembly to stand for the entire eucharistic prayer. Standing is the traditional posture for Christian prayer. It is the posture of the people of the resurrection and the posture of those who live in communion of life with God. And it is the posture of active participation and of covenant-making with the Lord. When the community remains standing, the unity of the prayer is better preserved and, because there is less disruption, everyone's attention to the text is maintained. Encourage the assembly to bow when the presider genuflects at the table.

Any discussion of posture will depend on whether or not there is local legislation governing the matter. The General Instruction of the Roman Missal (*GIRM*) (art. 21) indicates that the assembly "should kneel at the consecration unless prevented by the lack of space, the number of people present, or some other good reason." A number of good reasons have been given in the preceding paragraph. If the community has been kneeling for the institution narrative, it should stand to take part in the memorial acclamation, which can be sung properly only when the people are standing.

During your discussion, the question of respect needs to be addressed. In our culture, standing is the posture that we assume in the presence of leaders and dignitaries; in terms of liturgical protocol, it is the posture we assume for the rite of communion (See *GIRM*, # 21).

• discuss the possibility of inviting all the participants to extend their hands in a posture of prayer during the proclamation. It seems that in earlier times everyone in the assembly prayed in this manner. This will reinforce the assembly's ownership of the prayer and further draw the whole person into the celebration.

• work toward a full musical integration of the eucharistic prayer. The ideal is to sing the whole prayer; the presider's intoning line and cadences naturally lead into musically-integrated acclamations.

• constantly strive for a unified prayer. Since the eucharistic prayer is always in danger of becoming fractured, it requires constant attention to maintain its natural rhythm and its momentum towards the doxology and the Great Amen.

• use the eucharistic prayers as a source for reflection much as scriptures are used. This is an excellent way to move more deeply into the inner riches of the liturgical texts.

## In Summary

1. The eucharistic prayer is the table blessing of the feast.

2. It is the great prayer of the people of God. When liturgy is at its best, it will shine forth in all its beauty and richness.

3. The eucharistic prayer needs to be prayed with fervour. It deserves to be sung. Above all, it is, and must always be, the prayer of the entire assembly of faith.

## Discussion Questions

1. The eucharistic prayer should stand out as the great prayer of the church's feast. Discuss ways to strengthen the focus of this prayer in your parish celebrations.

2. The eucharistic prayer is the prayer of the entire assembly and of the whole church. Examine your parish celebrations and explore ways to draw the assembly more effectively into the prayer.

3. The eucharistic prayer needs to be prayed from the heart. In your parish celebrations, does the prayer ring out with the conviction of faith, or does it sound too much like a recited ritual text? What needs to be done to improve its proclamation?

4. It is no easy task to make sure that the table blessing is prayed as a single, unified prayer. When the eucharistic prayer is prayed in your parish celebrations, does it hold together well? What problems do you notice? How can you correct them? Do the musical components (for example, the acclamations) help to hold the prayer together?

# CHAPTER 4

# Holy Communion: Feasting at the Table of the Lord

Every household knows the pattern of a feast. The table blessing leads to eating, drinking and sharing life. Similarly, when the household of God gathers at the table of the Lord, the eucharistic prayer leads forward to holy communion, the heart of the church's sacred meal. Here are the main features of the celebration:

- the Lord's Prayer and the sign of peace;

- the breaking of the bread;

- sharing the holy food and drink, the body and blood of Christ.

## *The Lord's Prayer and the Sign of Peace*

Before the community shares the food and drink of the Lord's table, it needs to make sure that there is genuine peace in the household, that nothing holds people apart. The Lord's Prayer, which is a call to forgiveness, leads into the exchange of the sign of peace.

### Liturgy planners can ...

• discuss the quality of the assembly's participation in the Lord's Prayer with the parish presider(s). If the presider takes the lead, setting a firm measured pace, the assembly will follow suit, opening the way for a fervent recitation of the prayer.

• discuss the possibility of inviting the assembly to pray the Lord's Prayer with hands extended.

• examine the quality of the exchange of the peace of Christ and discuss ways to ensure that it is carried out in an honest, deliberate way.

### Music ministers can ...

• sing the Lord's Prayer only if the eucharistic prayer has also been sung and the community can sing it well. Never change the text to fit the music or leave the assembly with only a refrain to sing. If the Lord's Prayer is sung, the doxology (For the kingdom ...) is usually sung as well.

• take part in the sign of peace with others in the assembly at this time.

## *The Breaking of the Bread*

 "The breaking of the bread" seems to have been the earliest description of the church's eucharist. In the Acts of the Apostles we read, "Day by day, as they spent much time together in the temple, they broke bread at home ..." (2:46). The gesture is highly symbolic: the one holy bread is broken so that the many who share it may become one in Christ.

### Liturgy planners can ...

• restore the breaking of the bread to its original form and carry it out with care. The gesture of breaking the bread all but disappeared when small, pre-cut hosts came into use. Unfortunately, this coincided with a growing individualism in the communion rite. The ancient practice reinforces the corporate action of eating and drinking—of a people entering into communion of life with the all-holy God.

• discuss inviting communion ministers to approach the altar at the end of the eucharistic prayer and before the communion rite begins. The presider would then begin the Lord's Prayer after the ministers are in place.

Nothing in the liturgy has ever suggested that communion ministers should wash their hands at this time. It is true that the presider washes his hands before praying the eucharistic prayer, but this is a ritual gesture that reflected Jewish practices of purification before praying on behalf of the community. It is better to wash hands in the sacristy, if necessary, before the celebration begins.

## Music ministers can …

• sing the Lamb of God throughout the breaking of the bread and add additional invocations as required.

• perform the Lamb of God, which is a litany, as a litany. A cantor or the music group sings the invocation; the assembly sings the response. The final response, at the close of the breaking of the bread, is always "Grant us peace."

• select a setting of the Lamb of God that reflects the confidence and assurance of a people called by God in love.

The Lamb of God is sometimes taken to be a kind of plaintive chant begging God's mercy, but this is a misunderstanding of mercy. Mercy is God's gracious loving-kindness, freely and lovingly bestowed on a world that cannot in any way earn or deserve it. This loving-kindness reaches its full expression in holy communion.

### Communion ministers can ...

• keep in mind that breaking the bread is much more than a practical action. If you are called upon to assist in the breaking of the bread be sure to break the bread in a dignified way.

• be prepared, when there is no deacon, to pour the consecrated wine from the carafe into other chalices brought to the table by servers after the exchange of peace. Use a purificator to ensure that the consecrated wine does not spill onto the altarcloth.

## Sharing the Holy Food and Drink

Feasting at the table of the Lord is the high point and culmination of the eucharist, the goal towards which the entire celebration has moved. All sorts of profound thoughts come into play here: sealing the new covenant with God in the body and blood of Christ; making passage with Jesus through his death and resurrection into the life of glory; eating and drinking at the banquet feast of the kingdom; becoming what we eat and drink— the bread of life and cup of joy for our broken world; celebrating communion of life with the triune God.

### Liturgy planners can ...

• try to make holy communion a truly celebratory event that captures the spirit of a people eating and drinking together at the feast of new life.

• ensure that this part of the liturgy is not rushed.

• as much as possible, bring the people to share in holy communion at the altar, the one table of the Lord, where the assembly shares the food and drink the Lord offers. When this is not possible, establish communion stations relatively close to the altar. Avoid bringing communion to the back of the church.

• keep the procession for communion from becoming too regimented. Some good order is required, but using ministers of hospitality to move communicants pew by pew offends the familial nature of the eucharist. Use ministers of hospitality only with discretion, and look for other ways to ensure proper order.

• encourage communion from the cup whenever possible. The Lord himself told his disciples to take and drink, words which are repeated at every eucharist.

Avoid communion by intinction (dipping the consecrated bread in the cup). It fails to meet the prescription of the Lord to take and drink; it requires the minister to dip the consecrated bread in the cup and place it on the tongue. It is important to note that communicants are not permitted to take the consecrated bread and dip it in the cup themselves. The church's constant tradition is that communion is *given*.

• discuss the possibility of inviting the assembly to stand throughout the communion procession. The *General Instruction of the Roman Missal* (article 21) calls for the standing posture at this time. Standing is the posture of covenant-making; each person comes forward to seal the covenant until the entire assembly has renewed itself as the New Testament church.

• help the community, through bulletin inserts or workshops, to understand the covenantal nature of holy communion. The standing posture is the posture of covenant-making. The words of the rite, "The body of Christ. Amen" – "The blood of Christ. Amen", are a covenantal formula. Our "Amen," spoken in the midst of the assembly, is our commitment to give our lives in Christ for the sake of the world. When the whole assembly has made its vows, it stands renewed as the New Testament church.

• try to establish a pattern of bringing communion to the sick from the Sunday eucharist.

• consider the three options for the period that follows communion and consider which one is best for your parish community: 1) the community may observe a period of silence after everyone has shared in communion and before the prayer after communion is prayed; 2) a hymn of praise or a psalm may be sung; 3) the presider may call the assembly to prayer (Let us pray) after everyone has shared in the body and blood of Christ, with a significant pause for silent reflection before the prayer is prayed.

• arrange a proper way to consume the remaining elements, preferably after the celebration has been completed. Communion ministers may gather at the side table for this, or the remaining elements may be taken to the sacristy. Afterwards, the plates and cups are cleansed.

• ensure that any announcements are made after the prayer after communion has been prayed. Since this prayer brings the communion rite to a close, it is important to the integrity of the liturgy that announcements do not intervene between the procession and the prayer.

## Presiders can ...

• keep a single plate and a single cup on the table until it is time to divide the elements. After the exchange of peace, servers can bring extra plates and cups (with their purificators) to the table, if they are required.

• observe a significant pause for silent prayer after "Let us pray" when it is time for the prayer after communion.

## Communion ministers can ...

• see yourselves as servants of the Lord's table. There can be no greater privilege than this.

• share in communion before going about your work. Holy communion is the sealing of the covenant; you should do this yourself before you help others do the same.

• remember that this is the great feast. Be warm, welcoming and engaging. And be sure to smile.

• never rush communicants. This is the high point of the celebration and a time when both ministers and each communicant need to be personally present to the sacred action. Communion takes its own time.

• if you are ministering the consecrated bread, wait until the communicant is in place and properly composed.

• work out suitable arrangements for communion stations. If you are ministering the cup, be careful to stand some distance away from the minister with the consecrated bread. This will allow sufficient room for communicants to move from one minister to the next. Once again, wait until the communicant is in place and properly composed.

• carry the small amount of the consecrated bread that will be reserved for viaticum (communion to the dying) to the tabernacle in the chapel of reservation. Be sure to do so with dignity and decorum. The common practice is to genuflect after you open the tabernacle door and again before you close it.

## Music ministers can ...

• select music that everyone will sing. Nothing supports the communal dimension of holy communion more than singing together throughout the rite. Look for a psalm or hymn with a recurring refrain. Extend the song, if necessary, by instrumental interludes between the verses.

• avoid selecting two songs in place of one. A single psalm or hymn more effectively preserves the unity of the communion rite. Avoid singing a short hymn followed by a choral presentation.

• choose music that matches the rite of communion. Communion evokes such themes as covenant, unity, peace, praise and thanksgiving, and joy. Avoid using the period of communion to sing seasonal devotional songs or other hymns unrelated to the action.

• select music that is truly joyful, for holy communion celebrates the reunion of the world with God. Make sure that the song is strong enough to support the procession.

• begin the communion song when the presider begins the sharing in holy communion. In this way, the song envelopes the whole of communion.

• share in communion by joining the procession a few at a time. This arrangement allows the music to continue throughout the rite. If this is not possible, share in communion at the end of the procession.

## A special note for ministers of communion to the sick ...

• The best time to approach the altar is after you have shared in holy communion.

• After the presider has returned to the altar, he will fill the pyxes and hand them to you. Whenever you receive the consecrated bread destined for others, the whole assembly is reminded of the importance of uniting the sick members of the community to itself and to the Lord.

• Depending on parish arrangements, you may leave immediately or, perhaps better, take part in the closing procession.

## *In Summary*

1. Dining at the table of the Lord is the culmination of the church's feast, the goal toward which the entire liturgy has moved.

2. In holy communion, the assembly is renewed as the body of Christ and offers its life for the sake of the world.

3. In holy communion, we share communion of life with the triune God. In holy communion, we find our fulfillment and our joy.

## *Discussion Questions*

1. The Lord's Prayer and the sign of peace prepare us for holy communion. Discuss the quality of these liturgical acts in your parish celebrations. How can they become more fervent and honest expressions of our faith?

2. The breaking of the bread is a highly significant liturgical act. From our sharing in the one bread, consecrated and broken, we become one in Christ. What can you do to highlight the breaking of the bread in your parish celebrations?

3. Communion from the cup (which is the cup of the new and everlasting covenant) is one of the central acts of the church's liturgy. Does your parish offer communion from the cup to the entire assembly? If not, discuss its importance and consider an appropriate plan of implementation. Don't forget catechesis!

4. Since feasting at the table of the Lord is the high point of the entire liturgy, holy communion deserves special attention. Examine your parish celebration. Is holy communion too mechanical, too impersonal, too private, too rushed? Or is it the time of the assembly's fullest joy and the time of genuine covenant-making with the Lord? What can you do to improve the quality of this part of the celebration?

# Fulfilled in Joy

Long ago, the prophet Isaiah gave us these encouraging words: "On this mountain the Lord of hosts will make for all peoples a feast of rich food, a feast of well-aged wines, of rich food filled with marrow, of well-aged wines strained clear" (Is.25:6). The church's eucharist is that feast!

In this booklet, we have explored the richness of the liturgy of the eucharist. As the church's central act of self-identification, it tells us who we are. It reveals us as the body of Christ and the temple of the Holy Spirit, as a communion of life in the triune God. It identifies us as a people whose very life is to celebrate God in joy.

No doubt, we have sometimes hidden this truth about the church in the back of our minds. Sometimes we have tried to be something else. But in this age of renewal, it is all coming to light once again.

Yet, to change our way of life is not an easy thing to do. It means we have to change our vision. Jesus ascended into heaven, but he did not leave us. The risen and glorious Lord is present in our midst. We live in him and he lives in us. The eucharist tells us that it is so.

The kingdom of God is not only far beyond the horizon. It is already in our midst. It is not here in its full stature and shape, but it is really here. The Holy Spirit is even now at work in the world, transforming it and making it into something new. The eucharist tells us that it is so.

We are a celebrating people because we know that the Lord is with us. This very day he calls us to the feast of kingdom life. It is he who gathers us together, who speaks to us from the heart, who presides at the table, who shares his life with us in holy communion. It is all of this that lifts our hearts in thanksgiving and praise to our God.

The eucharist issues a challenge to our faith. Can we really believe that the Lord invites us to dine with him even now? Can we let go of all our fears and inhibitions and run to him in joy? Friedrich Nietzsche, the German philosopher, once said, "The trick is not to arrange a festival, but to find people who can enjoy it." What he said is true.

It is the experience of the feast, of sharing table fellowship with the Lord, that impels us outward on our mission in the world. What we have shared belongs to all; and we want everyone to share our joy. The *Constitution on the Sacred Liturgy* puts it well: "The liturgy is the summit toward which the activity of the church is directed; at the same time, it is the fount from which all the church's power flows" (10).

If the world has not yet accepted the good news of salvation, is it perhaps because we have not shown it a life of celebration and joy? This is the life that fulfills the yearning of the human heart. It is the witness of a celebrated life that leads the world to the joy of the cosmic dance.

What the world needs most is a feast of faith, a festival of new life, a celebration of rediscovered joy. What the world needs most is a place at the table of the kingdom of God. Let us taste its goodness now; and as we do so, let us remember the wise words of Joseph de Maistre: "Reason can do no more than speak; it is love that sings" (*Prières et poésie*, Paris, 1926).

## GLOSSARY

**Altar:** The church has always used a table for the sacred meal. When the veneration of the saints became very popular, it became customary to enclose the bones of martyrs in the base of the table, and the table itself took on the shape of a tomb. Today, the traditional form of the table is being gradually restored.

**Assembly:** The Latin word *ecclesia* may be translated either as assembly or as church. The term assembly denotes an officially convoked gathering, and is generally preferred to congregation. The Christian assembly is convoked by the risen and glorious Lord.

**Corporal:** (from the Latin *corpus*, meaning body) is a large cloth spread at the centre of the table for the liturgy of the eucharist. It used to be folded so that it would fit on top of the cup for transport to the table, but this is no longer necessary. The corporal is placed on the table during the preparation of the altar and gifts.

**Cross:** The processional cross is the original cross used in liturgical celebration. For many centuries it was either plain or richly decorated with jewels marking the place of the nails. In the Middle Ages, when an image of the crucified Christ was affixed to it, it came to be called a crucifix. Today we are witnessing a gradual return to the use of the jewelled or plain cross, which reflects the passage of Jesus through death to glory.

**Cup:** derived from the Latin *calix*, which simply means cup. Cup is used more commonly in English today.

**Eucharist:** (from *eucharistia*, the Greek word for thanksgiving) the traditional title for the church's principal sacramental celebration. By way of derivation, it can also be used to designate the consecrated bread and wine. The term mass, which is of much later origin, is taken from the Latin *missa*, meaning dismissal.

**Paten:** derived from the Latin *patina*, which simply means plate. Plate is used more commonly in English today.

Purificator: a narrow cloth used to purify the lip of the cup after a communicant has shared in communion. It used to be made of starched linen, but with the return of communion from the cup for all, it needs to be made of absorbent cloth.

Pyx: derived from the Greek *pyxos* and the Latin *pyxis*, which mean box. It is an enclosed container for the consecrated bread that is carried to the sick. As the shape of the bread used for the eucharist changes, the shape of the pyx may have to change as well. And as communion to the sick begins to include the consecrated wine, a suitable vessel will have to be found for it as well.

Sacrament: derived from the Latin *sacramentum,* meaning an oath of allegiance. All the other sacraments of the church are effective signs of the new covenant between God and the world sealed in the Lord's death and resurrection. As effective signs, sacraments bring about what they signify. Their power lies with the risen Lord, whose presence suffuses their celebration. It is he who acts in the power of his Spirit.

Sacramentary: the service book used at the table and the chair. It is positioned on the table so that it does not obstruct the assembly's view of the bread and the cup.

Sacrifice: has its roots in two Latin words, *sacer* and *facere,* meaning to make holy. It refers to the passover or saving death and resurrection of the Lord.

Sanctuary: (from the Latin *sanctuarium,* meaning holy place) describes the area surrounding the table. Today, it is often integrated within a unified celebration space. In a wider and more fundamental sense, the assembly itself, gathered around the table, is the sanctuary or dwelling of the Lord.

Tabernacle: derived from the Latin *tabernaculum,* meaning tent. The tabernacle houses portions of the consecrated bread that have been reserved primarily for communion for the dying. Today, the tabernacle is often located in a separate chapel of reservation.

BIBLIOGRAPHY

## *Recommended Reading*

*General Instruction of the Roman Missal,* Fourth edition (1975). This document contains the official legislation that guides the celebration of the eucharist in the Roman rite. The sacramentary includes it in its introductory material, and the Canadian Conference of Catholic Bishops also publishes it as a separate volume.

*Guidelines for Pastoral Liturgy.* This booklet is published annually by the Canadian Conference of Catholic Bishops. It includes extensive pastoral notes and a complete calendar for the liturgical year. Parishes usually keep a copy of the *Guidelines* in the sacristy.

Adam, Adolf. *The Eucharistic Celebration: The Source and Summit of Faith.* Collegeville, MN: The Liturgical Press, 1994. After examining the historical development of the Mass, Adam explains each part of the Mass in understandable terminology.

Cantalamessa, OFM Cap., Raniero. *The Eucharist, Our Sanctification.* Collegeville, MN: The Liturgical Press, 1993. With frequent reference to scripture and the church Fathers, Father Cantalamessa provides a meditation on the eucharistic mystery.

Emminghaus, Johannes H. *The Eucharist: Essence, Form, Celebration.* Collegeville, MN: The Liturgical Press, 1997. In this classic, Father Emminghaus traces the biblical roots and historical evolution of the mass, and then analyzes and comments on the basic structure.

LaVerdiere, SSS., Eugene. *The Eucharist in the New Testament and the Early Church.* Collegeville, MN: The Liturgical Press, 1996. Father LaVerdiere examines what the New Testament tells us about the eucharist and how the eucharist provides an important experiential and theological resource for the gospel stories of Jesus' life, ministry, passion and resurrection, as well as for the development of the church.

imprimerie gagné ltée